AVOWED

Julie R. Enszer

Sibling Rivalry Press
Little Rock, Arkansas
Disturb / Enrapture

Avowed

Copyright © 2016 by Julie R. Enszer

Cover art and design by Anna Sudit
Author photograph by Charlie T. Photography, © 2011

All rights reserved. No part of this book may be reproduced or republished without written consent from the publisher, except by reviewers who may quote brief excerpts in connection with a review in a newspaper, magazine, or electronic publication; nor may any part of this book be reproduced, stored in a retrieval system, or transmitted in any form, or by any means be recorded without written consent of the publisher.

Sibling Rivalry Press, LLC
PO Box 26147
Little Rock, AR 72221

info@siblingrivalrypress.com

www.siblingrivalrypress.com

ISBN: 978-1-943977-24-6

Library of Congress Control No. 2016945236

This title is housed permanently in the Rare Books and Special Collections Vault of the Library of Congress.

First Sibling Rivalry Press Edition, November 2016

TO KIM,
AVOWING FIDELITY

POEMS

1.

11	Pervert
14	Wedding
15	At the New York Marriage Bureau
16	Reticent Brides
17	Connubial Hour
18	When the Rabbi Asks for the Envelope
19	When the Marriage License Arrives
20	Imperfect
21	The Great Loves of Our Lives
23	Wind Chimes

2.

29	Breasts
32	She Is Feeding the Birds
33	Testing Abraham
35	Anniversary X
37	Cruelty
39	The Marital Bed
42	Seeing Judith Butler Speak
43	Menopause
45	Walking
47	Bring Me Back

3.

53	Beginnings
54	Sweater
55	Bed
56	Closet

57	Dishes
58	Socks
59	Distress
60	Heredity
61	Rings
62	Apogee
63	Coincidental
64	Seventy
65	Judgment
66	Demur
67	Conjugal
68	Devoted
69	Perfume
70	Stolen
71	Reconcile
72	Desire

4.

77	Heartbreak
79	Unfaithful
80	Chuppah
82	What Binds Us?
83	Eliyahu Hanavi
85	Officiant
87	At the Immigration Window, Miami International Airport
90	Tea-Bagging
92	After Fifteen Years,
93	A Lesbian Fantasia on *Angels in America*
96	I Meet a Woman

1.

What I wouldn't give to find a soulmate
Someone else to catch this drift
And what I wouldn't give to meet a kindred

Alanis Morissette, "All I Really Want"

PERVERT

The week before my mother died
I went to a feminist theory seminar,
and even though I can describe myself
as nothing other than happily married,
I wanted another woman.
An old school butch—
the kind of woman who exudes lesbian
through every pore of her being,
the kind of woman who sits comfortably
with her legs apart, who stands
forcefully, both feet firmly on the ground,
the kind of woman we describe
as ballsy and, on occasion, a ball-buster,
the kind of woman whose eyes
sear femmes's bodies,
making our nipples hard,
our clits erect,
our pussies wet—
the kind of woman I desire.
It was not just that I admired
her power, not just that I appreciated
her sexual being walking through the world,
glancing at me, giving me the benefit of lust.
No, I had to indulge
in the full-frontal fantasy.
During two days of seminars,
I imagined her fist hungrily
inserted in my vagina,
her long fingers first stroking
my muscular walls, gathering
the rhythm of sex, opening me
to accommodate four fingers,
a thumb, squeezed into a fist;
I imagined how my body

would open for her, how my lips
would quiver when my body erupted
into orgasm. I imagined looking into her eyes
as the ripples of my orgasm
squeezed her tight fist more deeply
into my body. I imagined making
her core to my body, central in my life,
in the way that only sex and lust bring
two women together. I imagined sucking her nipples,
laughing with her in the afterglow.
I imagined how much she would want
me after I took her whole hand
inside me, and, though I do not
believe this, when my father called
to tell me about the bleed
in my mother's brain and how
I needed to come home to help him
with the work death entails,
to mourn with him,
to bury my mother,
though I do not believe this at all,
I could not help but think:
I caused my mother's death
with my lust. Her death was G-d's
punishment for being an avowed
homosexual, punishment for my desire
of someone outside marriage,
for my continual, unrelenting lust for women,
which my mother had condemned
since I was eighteen.
I could not help but see my mother
in death somehow justified
in her anger, in her continued disappointment
with my perversity. I could not help but
think: I am a pervert who caused
my mother's death.
I could not help but hear
her final, fatal words, crushing

the lust, the fantasy from the conference.
She knew all along I would kill her,
after death she hissed, *I told you,*
I told you so.

WEDDING

No cream puff dresses, no
attendants, no flower girls.
No one gives us away,
but some tradition:
we sign a ketubah,
break a glass, stand
before G-d and our
families, make promises.
No one wonders
after fifteen years
will we last?
Only we wonder
why does the state take
so long to catch up?

AT THE NEW YORK MARRIAGE BUREAU

We present passports—
federal documents—for a license
the nation will not recognize.

Outside rain is pouring
from cloudy skies. We marvel
at bureaucratic efficiency:

swipe and sign. Thirty-five
dollars deliver a document
for the rabbi to certify.

I think it means nothing.
Two days later, we celebrate with
family and friends, brunch, cupcakes.

Our marriage did not happen
at the Bureau but New York
State prompted it.

Weeks later, I whisper,
I was wrong. It is transformative.
The public declaration

of love, previously private,
intimate. Not the license, not
the ceremony; the state.

RETICENT BRIDES

After fifteen years, we eschew bridal traditions.
A registry seems unseemly with a house filled
to the rafters. White dresses, a deception.
We are in no position to be given away
by unwilling patriarchs. We do not
borrow anything, though we wear blue.
The tradition we embrace? Ceremony.
Words on the page, spoken by an unauthorized
celebrant, the only person with authority
to stand before us and invoke the presence
of G-d. A figurehead who affirms to us,
to our families, the gravity of this commitment,
who celebrates of our shared lives.
We break a glass. Mazel tov! We cry.

CONNUBIAL HOUR

Late in the day, some family
departed, I tell her,
I am too tired. This day of
marriage exhausted me. But
she insists. She will have
sex on her wedding day.
There will be no bloodstain,
no mystery, just relaxed intimacy
of long-time lovers. Afterward,
I doze. My wife's thick vaginal
mucus dries on my hands, my nose.
Later, friends gather. Marriage
consummated, we dine on Thai
take-out with sticky, sweet sauces.

WHEN THE RABBI ASKS FOR THE ENVELOPE

to mail the authorized application
to the Marriage Bureau,
after she has supervised
our signatures and signing
by witnesses, I say,
Oh, I can mail it.
No, that's my job, she intones
gleefully. And for a moment
I withhold the mail carrier, meekly
adding, *But I have a stamp.*
She laughs. I release the envelope
with reticence. That moment,
I lost all control; the beloved and I
no longer strangers under the law.

WHEN THE MARRIAGE LICENSE ARRIVES

two week later, I leave it
on the kitchen table,
thinking if the license is lost
the marriage would be invalid,
but my wife assures me
the license can be reissued easily.
It sits on the counter for days.
Finally, she takes it. Files it.
Another document to manage.
After years of waiting for
formal state recognition of
our life, our love, our relationship,
when I finally receive it, I recoil.
Is paper all that makes a marriage?

IMPERFECT

The ketubah doesn't quite fit
the mahogany frame:
an extra quarter inch
on top and bottom.
I should have had it
professionally framed.
Carefully, I fold the edges
around the cardboard backing.
Hanging on the wall
the error is invisible.
This is the secret of marriage:
things don't always fit.
Fold, adapt, squeeze
into form. Make do.

THE GREAT LOVES OF OUR LIVES

begin with the body.
Desire is physical:
the flutter of the heart
the nervous shake of a hand
the dilation of the pupils
hardening of nipples
thickening of mucus
within vaginal walls.

New lovers celebrate the body,
revel in hungry
explorations of the vast
expanse of skin,
each fold, each gentle
mound of flesh,
the thick soup of fluids
that lubricate lovemaking—
spit and cum—
everything is sensuous.

This is how it began
with my wife.
I still remember
those days of desire,
the musky scent
wafting from every
inch of our skin.

If greedy, hungry
lovers are lucky,
they will spend some inestimable
number of years together,
then, it will be all about
the body again: the body
and its breakdown.

The day my mother
comes home from the hospital,
after the surgeon amputated
all her left toes,
she cannot bear any weight
on her foot.
Her bladder leaks.
Together, mother and father
learn to test her blood sugar
four times a day and
inject two types of insulin.

Bodies again with their fluids.
Now the ones they excrete:
a leaky bladder,
a lax sphincter.
The body breaks down.
Love does not always remain,
but bodies bind us—
their desire
their fallibility
their messy connections
to all that is human.

WIND CHIMES

After our morning wedding,
we gather in the hotel room
to open gifts. My oldest friend—
we have not lived in the same state
since fourteen and keep
our confidences in letters,
handwritten, over thirty years
across continents and
time zones—takes notes:
gifts, names, carefully recorded
for future acknowledgment.
At fourteen I might
have imagined this day
if we had not known
what was painfully
clear: my relationship
would not be recognized
by the state. Oh, the world
has changed.

       Her gift is
foodstuffs from the small
Wisconsin town where she lives
and wind chimes. Thick,
metal tubes suspended
with fishing line. Beautiful.
I imagine them on our
back patio singing
in the summer.
Worried they are
an unusual gift,
she explains,
When we got married,
we received wind chimes;

*at the time, I thought
what a dorky present,
but now every time
I hear them
I think of the gift giver.
So I give them to you
with that wish:
I will always be present for you.*

For over a year, she is
audibly in my life.
Then one day—a letter—
divorce. Now I wonder,
but do not know how to ask,
what will happen—
not to your children
your dog
your house
your life—
I wonder
what do you feel
when you hear
wind chimes?

2.

Come to my window
Crawl inside, wait by the light of the moon

Melissa Etheridge, "Come to My Window"

BREASTS

One night, in college, I slept
with a friend. The sex more
for curiosity than desire, and
afterward we were wildly
uncomfortable. I remember
because I left my quilt
and had to retrieve it,
my best friend in tow
(in our late teenaged years
we still traveled in packs),
but this isn't about my
post-adolescent discomfort,
it is about my bed-mate's
breasts, each a different size—
one B and one D.

This was before I slept
with an Australian-born
woman, whose favorite book
was *Nightwood*. She fancied
herself Robin Vote; I didn't yet
know what that meant—
the destructive force of Alex
in Djuna's hands—how she
might have fancied me Nora,
which would have pleased me
had I not read to the end.
The Aussie, as I would come
to call her, was married to a man,
securing citizenship for her,
a plausible beard for him.
They hadn't seen each
other in many years. She had
a long-term female lover;

she said the relationship
was intimate but no longer
sexual, and at my age,
tender, though not young,
I didn't understand the vagaries
of love, the restiveness of
relationships. Her double bed
had black sheets and only
one pillow. It was unmade.
There were no soft lights
in the room, only an exposed
bulb overhead. I didn't stay
the night. Now I don't remember
her name, but I remember
her breasts, reduced with large scars
from the base of her nipples
to her rib cage. When she sat
or stood, they were covered,
but lying, the thick, darkened
tissue frightened me.
I wondered how large they were
before the medical intervention.

When I first saw the breasts
of the woman who would
become my wife, I was awed
by their size. My excitement
even giddiness at the pleasure
I was about to enjoy took her
aback, almost with shame.
Now she revels
in her ample bosom,
in the pleasure it brings me.

I will see other breasts
in this lifetime—casually
at the gym or bared with
bravado at dyke marches—

but I wish never to hold
another woman's breasts.
Never squeeze, caress, or suckle
another's nipples. I leave
that to others. Each night
we sleep between clean sheets,
the beloved and I. The top
tucked tightly with a hotel-
fold. A king-sized comforter
to pull back. Reading lamps
on either side. Four pillows,
stacked at the head of our bed.

SHE IS FEEDING THE BIRDS

Twice a week she comes home
from the job she hates
with a ten-pound bag of birdseed.

At lunchtime, I buy fifty-pound
bags of dog food for the puppy
who has hopelessly captured my heart.

She sprinkles seeds for the squirrels
and fills two feeders daily—one on a low branch
of the holly, one hung near the back steps.

I roll on the floor with the 120-pound
St. Bernard, brushing her, cleaning her eyes,
wiping slobber from her face.

Blue birds, cardinals, wrens gather at dusk,
gorging on seeds, shitting on the bench
where we used to sip cocktails.

The squirrels grow fat.
She says, *We don't talk any more.*
She says, *You love the dog more than me.*

The other day, she came home and birds,
singing outside the garage, welcomed her.
A squirrel ate a peanut from her hand.

TESTING ABRAHAM

Perhaps he fancied himself Abraham,
the father of nations, but found himself
the father of three daughters, one now
long dead, the other two with no plans
to propagate—I wonder if we are
a cruel disappointment until I learn,
had my Dad been born
ten or twenty years later, reached maturity,
post-Stonewall, he might have found
himself without family or at least
not with our family, my mother,
my sisters, and me. His family
might have been queer like my adult family,
which wouldn't have existed because
I wouldn't be though that isn't the point,
this is: when I was running
the gay and lesbian community center
there was one group I didn't understand:
the bi married men.
They met once a month,
there were literally hundreds of them,
and for the longest time
they were the only group to meet
on Saturday night. While
everyone else went to bars or concerts
or out on dates,
they gathered in secret, albeit
at the gay and lesbian center
where they would never tell us
their last names or even
a telephone number to contact the leader—
they always said they would call us to check in,
resolve problems, which they did,
regularly, quietly; still I didn't understand.

They had over three hundred and fifty men—
who were these men? why did they stay married?
were they really bisexual?
or just waiting to be gay?
what did their wives think?
did they have children?
so many questions and no answers,
not even after my sister
sneaked a peek at my father's email
on Christmas Eve and found,
well, I don't know what
exactly she found—
I never asked—
she just called me crying
and accusatory *did you know*?
did I know my father was gay
or bi or whatever you call it when a man has a wife
and an apparent erotic interest in other men?
Did I know?
Did I know?
I told her, *no, I didn't know*, which I didn't,
and I told her I was angry
that she read our father's email,
which I was, and that begat
a familial schism of Biblical proportions
in which I am just a scribe
who will bury this book and deny,
deny, deny all knowledge—
I'll pretend I'm Rebecca, daughter
of Bethuel, son of Nachor,
whom Milcah bore to him,
a stranger in a strange land
until I am drawn
into this family drama again.

ANNIVERSARY X

The week before we celebrate
I am traveling for work.
From a friend's apartment
on the Upper West Side,
I walk around the corner
to café Margaux where I speak
with a French accent
(which everyone must know is fake
given my broad Midwest twang,
my earnest round face).
I almost don't want to return
to the suburbs
to my wife but I do.
I return home
to celebrate anniversary X,
though Malcolm may not approve—
he didn't live to see the fruits
of our revolution (not to mention his)—
but I take Malcolm's moniker
from his rejected patronym.
(Or should I say caucanym?)
At first glance it passes
as a right and proper Roman
but I think of it as X
as in X marks the spot,
stands in for all that is forbidden,
because, while we've been fucking
for ten years and are as intertwined
as any connubial couple,
we're not married
never have been and
at this rate never will be,
so I was going to plan a party
to cash in on the gifts we have given

over these many years to family and friends
but there is nothing we need
and my anniversand's mother died this year
and what's so special
about a decade anyway?
The Rabbi's revere eighteen years
chai chai perhaps we'll celebrate
shanah chai in eight more years
perhaps we will perhaps we won't.
I don't want to lie.
This year we celebrate anniversary X,
a couple of days amidst the life
we've built together.
I return home from New York
exhausted and stressed
as is my *Dodi*.
Still we stay up late
we talk
we remember falling in love
ten years ago during those autumn days.
It seems more fragile now
than it did then.
This is what we celebrate.

CRUELTY

Once I had a girlfriend.
We lived together,
planned to build a life—
house, kids. But as I was making
these commitments, I knew
she was not the one. I knew
we would not endure. Still
I said *yes* and *yes* and *yes*.
Then, fancying ourselves
pharaoh's daughter, rescuing
Moses from the bulrushes,
we adopted a dog. A black
dog. We named him something.
I don't remember.... Abraham?
Maximilian? Yes, Max for short.
Neither of us had ever had
a large dog, though Max was scrawny,
he hadn't lived with a family.
He peed everywhere.
Nervous and skittish,
perhaps sensing something
was wrong. After less than a week,
we called the rescue, confessed
our failure. Our relationship ended
within days of the dog's return.

I hope Max found a good home,
a loving home; I hope
he lived a long life.
I cringe, remembering my cruelty,
especially now that my most beloved
and I have rescued a new dog.
A St. Bernard. She's adolescent
and gawky—she cannot control

her large body—sometimes she nips
at my hands, my elbows, my hips.
She eats like a horse.
I think of her as a pony,
coaxing her to eat carrots.
I love her. That head-over-heels
kind of love, unabashed,
beyond all reason.
Today, I fancy myself,
not pharaoh's daughter,
but Zipporah. Mother of Moses.
She put him in the river,
then was summoned to nurse him.
I hold this orphaned dog
at my breast wishing for milk
to nourish, hoping a simple act
will atone for past sins.

THE MARITAL BED

I.

Driving home after the funeral I say,
I am peckish. We stop at 7-11 for fuel
and snacks. I want to tell you,
when the grandchildren
read from First Corinthians—
Love is patient, love is kind—
your aunt leaned over, whispered,
That was my mother's favorite passage.
We read it at our wedding.
Here she paused and pressed
the fold in the funeral program.
I would read it to Hugh
on every anniversary
until... well... you know.
Her voice tapered off and,
being in the middle of a funeral service,
we fell into silence. I wish I knew the New
Testament better to offer her words
of comfort; I wish I knew her sacred
scriptures for something to heal
her relational rupture,
but sitting in G-d's house,
we were alone and silent
watching the procession
of another's faith, the memory
of her life. *Comfort ye.*
Comfort ye, my people.
I can hear baritones
intone this message
for the holiday Messiah,
but here in this chapel,
she and I are both waiting.

Comfort ye. I don't
tell you any of this.

II.

Many years ago, one
of our dogs ate the fitted
sheet off the mattress.
When we came home,
it was tattered and torn.
For three days, he shit
partially digested
burgundy cotton. At the time,
those sheets were new
and the most expensive ones
I'd ever owned.
It took me a long time
to love him again.

III.

My sister is angry
about my father's affair.
*For forty years they slept
next to each other
every night with his lie
between them,*
she declares
with derision.
*That is probably
what made her sick,
brought on the stroke.*
My sister has not slept
with one person over
a period of years.
She doesn't know
the dailiness of sleep
with another. Its necessity.

Its urgency. How things happen
beyond explanation.
Sometimes my wife wakes
and shouts in anger;
some mornings,
she wakes in tears,
some days, before dawn,
before the mechanical alarm
beckons, before the cat's
hungry demands, I wake
with my belly pressed
to her back,
my hand on her hip,
the sheets at our shoulders,
our bodies shrouded with down;
I listen carefully to her breath,
steady, certain, secure.
Even forty years will never
provide enough days like this.

IV.

At the funeral,
I have yet to spend
three weeks in Mexico—
the longest we've been apart.
I do not know then
how by my final night away
I will be scheming
about how to organize
our lives so that we never
sleep apart again.
I think about your uncle,
returning home
from the hospital
after his wife died,
how wide and deep
the bed that night.

SEEING JUDITH BUTLER SPEAK

For five years, while reading
dense texts to make
my mind alert, my fingers
wandered to my clit,
my thoughts turned to you.
Until this day, unseen.
The perfect philosophic subject
for quick release then
return to turgid theory.
Now I see you live. In person.
Lesbian #9. Which is to say,
a lesbian type.
Hair, salt and pepper.
Jacket, black, leather.
Hands, unadorned.
As you speak
(already familiar with the printed
manner of your mind)
I study your mannerisms.
They are the same
as my beloved wife's.
In all those years of fantasy,
I never realized how close
you were at hand.

MENOPAUSE

Midlife I achieve
a complete set of crystal.
A gift from my wife.
Waterford. Champagne flutes.
Cocktail tumblers.
What I dreamed
in my twenties.
I circle the lips
make them sing
sonority erasing the absence
of nuptial rituals.
Two months later
while I dither about
emphatic instructions—
hand wash only—
my wife misses her period.
Sixty glorious days
absent bleached cotton
between her legs.
My menses inch
closer together
from twenty-eight days
to twenty-six.
This monthly act—
unconscious
unproductive.
No children born
of this union.
Lacking heirs,
I wash the crystal
in the dishwasher.
There is nothing
to protect.
I load them

on the top rack
like eggs
to ripen and release
into fallopian tubes.
Awash. Awaiting.
They imagine a future
nestled in utero.
Splitting, separating, growing.
A short cycle; they are done.
Ready to be retrieved,
safely stored in the cabinet.
Years of service and exposure
to sprayed water, extreme heat,
and detergent may
scratch or ding them.
They may become cloudy,
discolored, but like our eggs,
limited at birth, so is time.
This is how I choose
to spend mine.

WALKING

The pace of my life was set
walking with my father.
In high school, we walked
to school each morning.
He taught, I studied.
For three years, we watched
the seasons against the rhythms
of our steps. I learned to wear
practical shoes to keep pace
and gloves and hats and ear muffs
for warmth. I learned to carry
large books on my back, to engage
in early morning conversation.
In the fall we identified leaves
falling from the trees.
In winter, we waded through snow
and slush. Spring was marked by the
emergence of worms, splayed
across concrete; we stepped gingerly
to avoid them. Now he visits my
faraway home once a year.
We take long morning walks.
I tell him what I am reading:
histories of sexualities,
the emergence of gay identities.
He says, *Marriage wasn't always
about love and happiness. It was
once about commitment,
obligation.* He is fulfilling his,
and though I wish another life
for him, he is happy with his own.
The fourteen-year-old sophomore
inside me wants to make her father
happy—studying math and science,

reading all the great books of
the Western world—but I know
I'll never be the man my father is.

BRING ME BACK

you bring me back
like a robin in the spring
lift me up
help me spread my wings
like going home
down an old familiar street
you bring me back
back to the heart of me

"Bring Me Back" by Avenue Elle

For the first time
in sixteen years,
I hear a new folk
song about love,
devotion, kindness,
friendship,
and I think
of my wife
and not of you.

You and I have
spent more years
apart than we
were ever together.
You were my
friend, always
with the adjective
best. Today, I
do not know
the first thing
you see in the
morning, the last
book you read,

your favorite
new poem. Mary
Oliver has published
more than a handful
of books
that we have not
read together.

And now,
this song.
It should
make me think
of you. Don't
get me wrong,
I am happy
I thought
of my wife.
She is the one
who lifts me
up, who brings
me back, and
after sixteen
years, I owe
it to her to be
the first, the
last in my
heart, but
here I must
tell the truth:
there is still
some small
part of me
listening to
this song
that wants
me to think
first and last
of you.

3.

Highway run
Into the midnight sun
Wheels go round and round
You're on my mind.

Journey, "Faithfully"

BEGINNINGS

In Michigan, September dusk is chilly. We linger
in the parking garage of the downtown Millender Center.
Wind whips through concrete; the sun sets.
Cars cruise by. We identify makes and models
from internal combustion, the squeal of turning tires,
running engines. Our ears, expert at this exercise.
Neither wants to leave the other.
Polite conversation exhausted, we turn
to taboo: what we dream, secret hopes, desire.
We've touched only once when she brushed my hand
to light a cigarette. I tell her,
you must stop coming in my dreams.
Twenty-four hours later, each leaving
other lovers, we begin life together.

SWEATER

I am wearing a cream, cable sweater,
cotton with a cowl. It is my favorite.
First worn from the wash;
line dry required; often, too eager,
I wear it damp. Still shapen
and knit tight, it is formal
for meetings, comfortable
for gathering with friends.
Two years later, this sweater a sweet
reminiscence of our fall together,
until you spill oily food—salad dressing,
perhaps, a creamy alfredo. The sweater,
destroyed. No wash can clean it.
I never find a proper replacement.

BED

The first year even the best-made
beds in cold climes lie naked.
Sheets and covers cast aside.
Oil companies profit
on the backs of new lovers.
Once we would wake at five,
talk through sunrise, then rush to work.
Home again, we resume
what we regard as our real lives.
Later, early sojourns turn from intimate
discoveries to shared anxieties.
Phone calls pierce darkness
with bad news, and pillows,
matted or lumpy, absorb
more tears that muffled screams.
For a while, our angry cat, Gertie, pees
on the bed despite constant litter
cleaning and multiple vet trips.
Sometimes, between three and four a.m.
on a break from her game
of bridge, your dead mother visits.
I tell her about our life;
she strokes your hair and smiles.

CLOSET

In the hallway wearing only socks,
just as I drop my head to your shoulder
and you press your fingers toward contractions,
someone knocks.
         The dogs scuffle then break into canine song.

So soon after the breakup,
you whisper, *Oh, no, it might be her.*
Here—in the closet—
you hide me naked.

The floor is piled with shoes, bent hangers,
thin dry-cleaning bags.
In darkness, I root for a robe.
Then, laughter.

Meekly, you open the door. *This—is my friend—*I stick
out my hand, then draw it away. Musty, glistening with evidence.

DISHES

On our first Saturday together,
I tackle your kitchen.
Plates, pots, and pans piled
in the sink, on the counters,
in the stove. Too old to be rotten.
Just crusty, petrified. You advise,
Just throw out that pan;
I'll buy another.
But soap, hot water, and scrubbing
clean and shine them all.
Now I want to whisper
to my younger self:
Passion fades.
You will always be doing the dishes.

SOCKS

Your mother remembers meeting
your father when she was nineteen,
just days from prom queen. She tells me,
He was stunning, tall, athletic,
beautiful hair, and you should have seen
his socks—cashmere—.
Last Christmas, you gave me three pairs—
black, argyle, cream cable. They are perfect.
Soft, warm. But after three washes,
the heel is threadbare.
I imagine your mother
discovering this early in her marriage.
I wonder, what did she find
to hold that lasts?

DISTRESS

This is never captured by Hollywood:
anxiety after each of you leave
another to be together.
We spend years worried
about each new friend or
acquaintance. New evening activities—
political campaigning,
card clubs, poetry readings—
any late night out, leaves one
at home to wonder,
will the day come
when we rehash the well-trod line,
this is the best day of my life,
as it becomes the worst of mine?

HEREDITY

Anxiety, compounded by family history—
her father's first child born six months and
one year after he married her mother
(ten years before she was adopted)
and a quarter century before she,
at fourteen, picked up
the telephone to overhear
her father's amorous imbroglio.
Two years later, her parents divorce.
She declares to me her fealty,
but I worry, what if parents pass
infidelity like deoxyribonucleic
acids? What if our base pairs
contain our future affairs?

RINGS

Near Valentine's Day, we buy rings on a lark,
though we do not save them as gifts, just get them sized.
Mine, a permanent resident on my right finger;
Hers, an occasional embellishment.
When asked about marriage, I hold out
my left hand, bare. We say, we'll marry
when it's legal in our state. This makes me feel perfectly safe
until I hear of European tradition
that adorns the right hand with the wedding ring.
I think of continentals considering me married.
Customs are never easy.
Still, with no band—no initials and date inscribed—
we date our existence like scientists testing for
radiation emissions, marking half-lives.

APOGEE

The hardest year was seven,
not an itch but an irritation
that persisted.
I resented the repeated
need to shop,
run a household,
mostly the way she enjoys these things.
I wanted time for myself.
Now I see people at this point
in their marriage, they ask,
How did it pass? The truth
makes me look bad.
My lover's mother was sick and
suddenly her death was in sight,

and I, not wanting
to be the sort of woman who leaves,
tried to stop complaining
(she will tell you I didn't, but I tried).
I cleaned, made arrangements
for a dozen trips.
Hotel and rental car reservations.
Packed luggage with small gifts,
even assembled Easter baskets for mother and daughter.
We knew how the story would end.
I couldn't be the woman
who left another grieving.
By the time the veil of loss lifted,
we were honeymooning again.

COINCIDENTAL

When my sister reads my father's
email one Christmas Eve, she calls
me and demands, *Did you know?*
Did you know? As though queers
were some secret fraternity;
every member vetted, reviewed,
approved. She doesn't understand
how capacious the questions of sex.
My father met someone willing in his sixties.
I hope for the same virility,
but my sister is seething in anger,
my mother, in shock and disbelief, and
I admit I never expected my father
to want dick in his mouth, in his ass.

SEVENTY

Growing up too young to be
a child of the sixties, I am aware
that sex in the seventies was different,
somehow special, exciting,
and, aided by powerful antibiotics,
without fear or precautions.
While my homosex was tempered
by the specter of premature death,
some recall sex without inhibitions.
In this tradition, I think of sex in the seventies
with longing, even yearning,
until it becomes not sex in the seventies
but sex in one's seventies—
a concept I'm forced to consider

when my beloved's uncle
tells us he's been unfaithful to his wife
of thirty-some years.
More than relatives,
they were correlative:
marriage and happiness,
retirement and joy,
lovers and companions.
Now my aunt, reduced to mistrust and misgivings,
confides, *He's addicted to the oral sex.*
This makes me worry
someday the same accusation will be flung at me,
but for now only he's called
to account for these transgressions.

JUDGMENT

I quip to friends—
it's inspiring to see
untamed desire propagate
among the retired.
We'd like to imagine ourselves
horny at sixty-seven,
getting it on with a new one at sixty-eight,
committing cunnilingus at sixty-nine,
all foreplay to wild sex in the seventies.
Gales of laughter erupt all around,
but it's not true.
We're moralistic in our thirties and forties,
as shocked by their new adolescence
as they once purported to be by ours.

DEMUR

Now I wonder about our uncle's visits
to Thailand—R&R from the military.
I think of the person who gave me
a foot massage the week I was there.
He—or she—I couldn't tell—rubbed
my toes, my heels, my calves,
proceeded up my thighs
until I opened my eyes.
Thank you, I said. Then she—or he—
(I confess, I like to know gender;
it is central to my sense of orientation)
simply stopped.
Why did he, like me, not simply
open his eyes and say, *Thank you*?

CONJUGAL

When did we first demand exclusivity?
Who deemed it so? Surely not G-d,
the primordial polyamor. She loves us all.
Adam had the inaugural "starter" marriage,
leaving Lilith to enjoy her later days as a singleton.
The Torah tells the truth—
lust and love break down to betrayal—
G-d mocks us: you've been forewarned.
As though forewarned is forearmed.
As though there are armaments
to wage this war beyond our flesh,
beyond our feeble hearts
and wayward minds,
beyond our hungry tongues.

DEVOTED

For years I wanted to be my aunt:
direct, plain-spoken, clear about priorities.
Beginning with family but extending to a wide array
of social and ethical responsibilities.
And you, my beloved, I fancied you, your uncle,
enjoying the flurry of activities, occasional nattering.
One year, they took six cruises.
Visited every port on the planet,
but travel didn't bring them closer.
We fear it may never be enough:
miles, apologies, moral accounting.
We watch the unraveling, knowing now
we can be neither. We hold to one
another, though never too tightly.

PERFUME

Thirteen years since
my wife left you for me,
I think about the perfume
she bought you for birthdays
and anniversaries. My own
temples bare of sweet
scents from beautiful bottles.
You lined them atop your dresser.
I wonder about their fate.
Was there one day when you
sprayed the last drop?
Or on this day, our anniversary,
did you, in anger,
throw them all out?

STOLEN

Sometimes, rinsing the dishes as I load
the washer, sponging small pieces of lettuce,
clumps of parmesan cheese in creamy
Caesar dressing, I think this isn't my life.
It is the life I stole from you. I've made it mine—
installed a tile floor with grout (that needs
to be cleaned), purchased sturdy, daily dishes,
bought food with your money.
Cleaning the refrigerator, moving jars
and cans and bottles, bits of produce from the farm,
I take out the shelves, wash them in warm, soapy water,
replace the box of baking soda. I want this life to be clean,
free from odors, if you come back.
If you return to claim it.

RECONCILE

Everything that has brought me
to this moment in my life—
every movie I've seen
every book I've read
every philosophy I've espoused
every ideology I've studied—
tells me I should hate
this uncle, my father,
my beloved's father…
but I can't. All old men.
Ineffably human.
I am they.
Each day, I walk out the door.
It is a choice. How I return.

DESIRE

When I was moving every year,
you came with your truck
and a passel of butches
to transport boxes of books,
carry them up and down stairs,
counsel lovers I was leaving.
More than once you told me,
*This is the last time, Julie,
the last time*. Finally, it was
the last time. I have not seen
you since. Now twenty
years later, we each own houses,
live with lovers of many years.
Our lives are settled.

Still you have a large truck.
As I step up into it, we marvel
about all that has changed,
though this big Ford is the same.
And when you smile,
I still imagine wrapping my legs
around your ears,
how you might stroke my ass,
what your lips might lick,
how you might suck my clit
in the gap between your teeth.
This could be the reason
I've not seen you in decades,
the reason I should not see you again.

4.

"Love should be put into action!"
screamed the old hermit.
Across the pond an echo
tried and tried to confirm it.

—Elizabeth Bishop, "Chemin de Fer"

HEARTBREAK

Two hours before I must leave
for the airport, my wife says,
I am afraid I am going to die.
Shortness of breath.
Heart palpitations. I still only
want her heart to flutter
for me. She says, *I worry*
about the dogs if I have
to go to the hospital. Again,
I am afraid I am going to die.
I confide, *Me, too.*
Every night I fear I'll sleep
and not wake up, but
every morning, here I am.
We continue to live,
but hanging over the
conversation is the truth
we see in fragments:
one of us will die,
leave the other
as my mother left my father,
as cousin James
left his beloved Jane and she
observed plaintively,
language and movement
impaired by her body's failings,
He said he would always
take care of me. We have made
no such promises. We hold
more fiercely to independence
than reliance. Here in this moment
of grief, this moment of
fear, we know: one day
someone's heart will break.

There is nothing we can do.
I fly to San Francisco. Eight
days later she joins me.
For now, together, we stare
down fear, imagine a
life with strong, steady hearts.

UNFAITHFUL

Once I believed marriage was received,
separate from the self,
a third thing to which two people cleave.
Concrete—a large antique chest
not finely made, but utilitarian,
the kind that moves from farmhouse
to garage to first apartment.
Or long-lasting sheets, part polyester,
given to family members in need.
Marriage isn't like that.
As much as it's shared,
it's an individual burden
or gift—depends on the day—
like this morning,
I meet a gorgeous woman
wearing old Levis, a silk shirt
and suddenly I am my uncle,
sleeping with his brother's wife.
I am my father with a clandestine lover.
Indiscretion is easy.
Like the men in my family,
there is nothing to stop me.

CHUPPAH

Fresh out of college,
I wanted a mother
like those of my friends—
unloading used dishes
and pots and pans
into their daughters'
apartments as they replaced
their own, arranging to drop off
basement love seats
(from former family rooms
now converted for crafts
or work outs), perfect centerpieces
for first-time apartments.
My mother gave money,
bought me new towels.
The things I yearned for
from my childhood home—
the bedroom set, a side chair,
the desk her father made by hand—
they were hers.
She would not share.

Her mother died
when she was twenty-three.
She, like me, wanted things
from her childhood home—
dishes, her mother's sewing
machine and piano—but within a year
her father remarried.
His new wife had dominion
over the household.
She wanted the objects
mother coveted.

As a young woman,
lovers gave or bought
me things to furnish
my home—a couch, table
tape deck, many wooden
bookshelves. Their love
replaced what was lacking
from mother.

Now in the home
my wife and I share,
I have everything
I once desired:
matching daily dishes,
a separate set for formal
entertaining, wine goblets,
flatware to serve twenty,
pottery serving platters,
formal coffee service,
and aperitif goblets.
She and I built a home
together, piece by piece.

This is why we do not
marry under a chuppah:
our home already built.
This is why every day
I thank God
I was born a woman.

WHAT BINDS US?

Not bi-weekly sex
not ribbon wrapped around our wrists at a wedding
not the shared mortgage
not joint credit cards
not car notes
not even the dogs
all could be sorted, separated, split

Shared moments:
how you anticipate I will want to eat your pussy after watching Mary-Louise Parker
the funerals of many family members
the way I know you will return from work tired
not wanting to talk
until after you mix a martini
how when you walk through the door
you won't be hungry for dinner
but in forty-five minutes you'll be starving
how you sleep holding the television remote
how we dress for funerals
how you want me to caress your butt publicly
my bold femme move
your butch desire
how you want that when we are in our 50s our 60s our 70s

ELIYAHU HANAVI

I imagined Elijah a middle-aged castrati
until I read and find him to be young, virile
like Ajax—the strong man of the Heebs.

I think of my own father—the strong man
of my tribe. In the basement he bench-pressed
on a small, red carpet remnant; in summer,

he'd lift weights midday in the cool cellar.
He'd emerge red-faced, glistening with sweat.
Wintertime, warmed by the furnace, he'd heft

late at night. Below, his life was fully his own—
no intrusions from daughters or wife.
Now, far away from my parents' home,

the iron men in my life lift weights,
carve pecs, quads, and glutes in large, airy gyms.
They cruise and shower and shave

in well-lit, public spaces. I think of my father
in our dark basement—building the body
of a gay man in stark isolation.

For him, I take comfort in Elijah.
Perhaps with his Elijahic body,
G-d will give him two tries—

the Phoenician princess Jezebel, then
an Adamic lover. Maybe after forty days
in the wilderness, after being fed by ravens

in the desert canyon, G-d will say to my father,
Elijahic one, Arise and eat,

and perhaps with strength from the second meal,

my father will walk through the desert
of public gyms, bars, quiet dinner clubs
until he reaches the mount at Horeb

where a "still, small voice" may ask,
Ma lekha po, Eliyahu? Why are you here, Elijah?
And he may answer, *I am no better than my fathers.*

But if I am asked of him,
Ma lekha po, Eliyahu?
I will translate,

Who are you, here, Elijah?
and I will reply, *You are my father.*
I could want no better.

OFFICIANT

We struggled with who would marry us—
stand with us before the eyes
of G-d, recite some sacred words,
demonstrate to all gathered
the gravity of this moment.
It could not be a person
of the cloth, our religious affiliations
not oppositional but not congruent.
We decide on a friend—
theatrical, oratorical, powerful—
with the authority to marry us from
his own long term marriage.

A few year later a friend
asks me to officiate at his wedding.
He admires our marriage.
Then, I learn that Eric,
our officiant, is getting a divorce,
and I want to tell my friend:
No, I cannot marry you,
I know nothing of marriage,
but I cannot because
this is the nature of friendship:
support and celebration,
saying yes more often than no,
and because I reject
superstition—serving as
officiant does not lead necessarily
to divorce—though it did for Eric
and now I fear it will for me.
Then we have dinner with Eric
and his new lover and she is lovely
and I hate her, though I should not,
but there must be some line

I can draw. Say, here, this,
I will not transgress.

AT THE IMMIGRATION WINDOW, MIAMI INTERNATIONAL AIRPORT

Younger, when we traveled,
our bags were always frayed
or too heavy
or falling apart.
We crossed borders
with broken wheels;
we carried bulky duffel bags
that cut into our shoulders.
In airports and train stations,
I would see someone
traveling efficiently
with luggage that worked;
I wanted to be that person.
Occasionally, I would see
a lesbian couple
with matching luggage
astride at the airport,
and I would think,
that is my future,
that is what I want
my future to be.

Before we were married,
when we were just two broads
traveling abroad,
I always would suggest
we complete just one
custom's declaration.
The form bolstered my argument:
one per household.
My wife always demurred
but marriage emboldened her.

And so when we arrive at the
immigration window
off the plane from
San Jose, Costa Rica,
with fashionable handbags,
ready to retrieve our
matching Tumi luggage,
carefully packed so it rolls easily,
my wife drags me with her to the
immigration window with a single form
and when the officer asks,
what is your relationship, she says,
She is my wife.

I never imagined
we would be married,
expect federal agencies
to recognize us officially.
It was always me pushing—
only one customs form—
now when it happens
I recoil from this banter of wife,
from this formal recognition.
Suddenly, here in Miami,
I want to be illegal
      transgressive
        other
I want matching luggage.
I want to demand recognition
not have it given freely.
I mourn the loss of struggle.

We retrieve our baggage.
Luggage, not a burden of travel,
not a drag, an accent
to adventure. This is the life
I always desired: a long-term partner,
travel to sunny climes in January,

a single form delivered
with a flourish, the re-admittance
of our bags, of our bodies
to our native land.

TEA-BAGGING

I filed our taxes two months ago
so we marvel without stress
at the tea-bagging antics

of modern day tax protesters.
We revel in queerness and
on the eve of April 15th, we

join the celebration and
teabag, even if it's dubious
whether two women can.

Every dish in the house is dirty
from the spaghetti you made
for dinner. We are sated

by big meatballs, a blend of
veal, beef, and pork, baked, then drowned
in sauce, sweetened by sugar.

We've been aroused by the pleasure
of eating. We kiss and canoodle.
Suck on each other's breasts.

Then you lower your labia
to my lips. Moist, steeped
in sweat. I lick and flick

your clit. Suckle your labia
majora, which is changing,
not growing exactly, but

I notice differences as our years
together pass. Some days more nubile
and easily erect. Others

flaccid, even baggy. Tonight,
enlarged, engulfed. It presses
my nose as my tongue

shimmies inside your lips.
Not sac-like, never
the site of semen production,

your outer labia is like a tea cozy
warming, extending the heat
of a respite we might call

"tea-time." I laugh. I think
about taxes. How you feed me.
How we tea-bag.

AFTER FIFTEEN YEARS,

what is marriage?
A ceremony,
a party,
a document to be framed.
It doesn't change
the texture of daily life.
It doesn't lessen frustration
when I leave clothes
in the dryer to wrinkle;
it doesn't pay the bills,
replace the chimney cap
blown off in this summer's storm,
fix the slow leak in the A/C line
that runs in the crawl space overhead.
Somewhere a drip, drip, drip
is slowly discoloring the ceiling,
cream then brown.
The paint peels away,
and the spackle from the last repair
crumbles down onto our bed.
We are relieved that it is not
the roof. After the big fall rain
when the unit was off for the season,
no moisture.
Marriage will change none of this,
but it does make it
more difficult
this Monday morning
at 4 a.m.
to wrench my body
from our warm bed.

A LESBIAN FANTASIA ON *ANGELS IN AMERICA*

Louis, I fear I will be you
abandon the one I love
in a time of great need
though equal to my fear of
being Louis is my fear
of loving someone like Louis
of being Prior. Prior Walter.
Prior, prior, what was before
what we were before
what we loved before
this was our life prior.
Prior, so much easier than
future, after, what will be
the certainty of what was
even when it is a mystery
is one that can be solved
it happened in the past
Prior, it can be known.
Prior. I want to be Prior
the prophet the mystic
the visionary. Prior, who ascends
to the heavens
up a fiery ladder
and returns to earth through water.
Prior, elemental, earthen, airy, burning,
I burn for Prior.
I yearn for Prior.
Prior the man who represents
the hope of us all
the possibility of making meaning
from the epidemic,
the senseless loss of life
when a government looked away
without care.

Prior. I want to be Prior.
But I know I am Louis.
Broken, unable to
complete the Kaddish until Ethel
intones those ancient words
with him *Yit'gadal v'yit'kadash sh'mei raba*
though even these words bring
neither of them forgiveness
neither redemption.
Ethel, long dead
Louis, unable to be present
in the simplest of ways.
Reading a book about democracy,
Louis is unable to see the failings
of democracy before us today.
Yes, I am Louis, broken, unable
to hang in for the hard times;
even after sixteen years,
I doubt my ability to stay,
to be the loyal one,
and Kushner gives me no model
no hero
just anger at a G-d
who has abandoned us.
Every morning
I wake and see Louis's face
in the mirror.
Even today years later,
as we enter the teens
thirteen years
since the millennial turn,
millennium no longer approaches,
the millennium has passed.
Louis now in his sixties
and Prior, if he lived
until January 1996 now alive
happy, partnered, maybe married—
with a New York marriage

like mine—
we all grow up,
the millennium passed,
Perestroika not what we imagined
no ascent to heaven
no choice to return to earth
just daily life
arise each morning
mirror offers
little comfort
even the words
spoken at the fountain of Bethesda
provide little solace
though maybe this is
all there is
these words:
We won't die secret deaths any more
we will be citizens
the time has come
you are fabulous
each and every one
and I bless you
more life
the great work begins
these words
these sixteen years.

I MEET A WOMAN

Friday night, after a long day of work
and far away from home, I am at
an event to hear a friend speak
and sell her books. I am tired.
Exhausted really. All I want
is to return home to my lover,
our dogs, our life. Then, across the room,
I see a woman. The kind
I always desire: an avowed butch,
wearing a gorgeous suit,
curly, dark hair atop her head
(I can only imagine what is below),
confident, smiling, bewitching.
All night, from afar, I watch her;
finally, as the crowd dwindles,
we speak. She flirts,
marvels at how young I am.
Reader, I am not young, just
younger than she, and then,
only slightly. She touches my face.
My face! I giggle. I am young enough
for such girlishness but old enough
to know: I want my hand inside her.

My desire reminds me of this lesbian myth:
two women are making love. One
puts first a finger inside the other,
then two, then finally her full hand
inside the lover's vagina—
it slides in easily to the warm, wet,
engorged cave—you know how open
we become desiring, wanting, having another.
Then, when she comes, looking into the eyes
when she comes, she comes hard,

the contractions of her strong,
wet, vaginal muscles, squeeze
and squeeze so hard
a finger breaks.

It's a myth, but in this moment,
I want this woman to break my finger.
I think about her for days. How
my hand might fit inside her, how
she might enjoy it. How she might
touch my face again when she comes,
my whole hand inside her loveliness,
drenched and pulsing. How we might
both be young and giddy, breaking things
as we come again and again.
If I see her again, more will break
than a finger. Our carnal sex would fracture
or shatter more than a small digital bone.
If I see her again, we might destroy many lives.
I want to lay my hand inside her.
I want her to break my finger.
I want to break.

NOTES

The neologism, anniversand, in "Anniversary X" derives from words like analysand and multiplicand where something acts on something else. The anniversand is my partner, and the anniversary is acting on her.

"Eliyahu Ha-Navi" engages the story of Elijah in 1 Kings 19.

In "A Lesbian Fantasia on *Angels in America*," the quotation that concludes the poem, beginning "We won't die secret deaths," is from Tony Kushner's *Angels in America*.

These four poems are dedicated with great affection and love to the people who inspired them:

"Wind Chimes" is for Carrie
"Bring Me Back" is for Lis
"Desire" is for Carla
"Officiant" is for Eric

ACKNOWLEDGMENTS

I am grateful to the following journals, anthologies and editors for publishing these works, often in an earlier version:

Animal, "She is Feeding the Birds"
Beltway, " The Marital Bed
The Bloomsbury Anthology of Contemporary Jewish American Poetry, "Cruelty" & "Eliyahu Ha-Navi"
Blue Lyra Review, "Imperfect"
Gargoyle, "Breasts"
Glitterwolf, "Menopause," "When the Rabbi Asks for the Envelope"
Jewrotica, "Seeing Judith Butler Speak"
Lady Business, "Beginnings," "Sweater," "Bed," "Closet," "Dishes," "Distress," "Heredity," "Rings," "Apogee," "Coincidental," "Seventy," "Judgment," "Demur," "Conjugal," "Devoted," "Perfume," "Stolen," "Reconcile," "Unfaithful" (titled then "Coda")
Milk & Honey: A Celebration of Jewish Lesbian Poetry, "Testing Abraham"
Nimrod, "I Meet a Woman"
OCHO, "A Lesbian Fantasia on *Angels in America*"
The Quotable, "Tolerance," "Dress"
Rattle, "Pervert"
The Rumpus, "The Great Loves Of Our Lives"
Skin to Skin, "At the Immigration Window" and "Menopause"

Thank you to early readers Cheryl Clarke, Reginald Harris, Jenny Factor, Lawrence Schimel, Gerald Maa, and Michael Walsh. Even more thanks to Cheryl Clarke and Michael Walsh who substantially improved individual poems and the full manuscript. Seth Pennington's copyedit and initial feedback also improved the flow of these poems.

Gratitude to Bryan Borland and Seth Pennington for their fine work as writers and publishers.

Love always to Kim and our pack, Emma, Vita, and Tiberius; while finishing the manuscript, Tibe reminded us all about the meaning of home.

ABOUT THE POET

Julie R. Enszer is the author of *Lilith's Demons* (A Midsummer Night's Press, 2015), *Sisterhood* (Sibling Rivalry Press, 2013), and *Handmade Love* (A Midsummer Night's Press, 2010). She is editor of *Milk & Honey: A Celebration of Jewish Lesbian Poetry* (A Midsummer Night's Press, 2011). *Milk & Honey* was a finalist for the Lambda Literary Award in Lesbian Poetry. She has her MFA and PhD from the University of Maryland. Enszer edits and publishes *Sinister Wisdom*, a multicultural lesbian literary and art journal, and is a regular book reviewer for the *The Rumpus* and *Calyx*.

ABOUT THE PRESS

Sibling Rivalry Press is an independent press based in Little Rock, Arkansas. It is a sponsored project of Fractured Atlas, a nonprofit arts service organization. Contributions to support the operations of Sibling Rivalry Press are tax-deductible to the extent permitted by law, and your donations will directly assist in the publication of work that disturbs and enraptures. To contribute to the publication of more books like this one, please visit our website and click *donate*.

www.ingramcontent.com/pod-product-compliance
Lightning Source LLC
LaVergne TN
LVHW041342080426
835512LV00006B/572